WORKBOOK FOR LIVE NOT BY LIES

Copyright © 2021

All rights reserved. No part of this publication may be reproduced, stored in a retrieval system, or transmitted in any form or by any means (including electronic, mechanical, photocopying, recording, or otherwise) without prior written permission from the publisher

Note to Readers

Legal Disclaimer/Limit of Liability: Effort has been made to ensure that the information in this book is accurate and complete, however, the author and the publisher do not warrant the accuracy of the information, text and graphics contained within the book due to the rapidly changing nature of science, research, known and unknown facts and internet. The Author and the publisher do not hold any responsibility for errors, omissions or contrary interpretation of the subject matter herein. The use of this book implies your acceptance of this disclaimer.

This book is not meant to replace the original text but is designed to ac-company the original work: *"Live Not by Lies: A Manual for Christian Dissidents by Rod Dreher"*

This is an unofficial workbook meant for educational, personal and informational purposes only. The advice and strategies contained herein may not be suitable for all situations. This book has not been authorized, approved, licensed, or endorsed by the author of the original book or his/her publisher and any of their licensees or affiliates

Companion books are legal and our intention in publishing this book is sincere, in that readers can use this book as a companion to the original book, not as a substitute.

THIS BOOK BELONGS TO

_____

_____

HOW TO EFFECTIVELY USE THIS WORKBOOK

This book is a companion book to *"Live Not by Lies: A Manual for Christian Dissidents by Rod Dreher"*

With this book, you can accelerate your personal development and get a much deeper understanding of each section of the main book.

This book is to be used alongside the main book. After going through each section of the main book, you dedicate some time to work through that same section in this book.

With this book, there're no judgments and you are free to express yourself as truthfully as you can as you stretch your limits and break mental, emotional and other barriers to achieve the impossible

Do not rush in answering the thought-provoking questions. Some questions can be skipped to be returned to at a later time.

INTRODUCTION

In his book, **Rod Dreher** explores and questions what is happening around us today and the different changes that are as a result of a gradual and steady shift towards a totalitarian nation.

When the Berlin Wall fell in 1986, so did the Soviet totalitarianism and communist police that that had enslaved Russia and over half of Europe.

As the Cold War ended, it was now time for democracy and capitalism to blossom in nations that had previously been held captive, pushing totalitarianism into oblivion.

However, in today's world it seems life is gradually drifting towards totalitarianism as the Lefts try to control thoughts and discourse, labelling any dissenter as evil and marginalizing them.

Driven by a utopian vision, these progressives are trying to rewrite history and reinvent language that suits their ideals of social justice, and seek to create a powerful mechanism to control thought and discourse.

They constantly change their standards of thought, speech, and behavior, and even more troubling is the fact that most Americans and the rest of the West don't recognize what is happening right before them.

His research helps you;

- Identify and resist totalitarianism in our present time.
- Understand the influence of soft totalitarianism on the modern man.

- Overcome the psychological manipulation of totalitarianism
- Protect the truth through the actions you take
- Identify those areas of life where identity politics has encroached into.
- Handle pressure without folding
- Become more productive and joyful
- be more of yourself
- have meaning in your life

PART ONE
Understanding Soft Totalitarianism

CHAPTER ONE
KOLAKOVIĆ THE PROPHET

KEY TAKEAWAYS & CRUCIAL POINTS

- Modern day Americans are mostly blinded towards the effects of totalitarianism.
- Unlike the old totalitarianism of the Soviet Union, the new, soft totalitarianism has a deeper and more encompassing effect because this time, we are actively making room for it.
- Comfortability has become the primary goal of the modern man, secondary to no other desire.
- The task of Christians today is to commit to a life of truth.
- To live by lies is to denounce all that you believe to be true and to accept willingly the lie that affords us a life more convenient.
- Living in truth can be a lonely stand, but as Christians, it must be considered a necessity.
- Therapeutic culture has its claws deep into the world, and Christians have gradually adopted this culture.

QUESTIONS

In what ways have you experienced totalitarianism?

_____
_____

_____

_____

_____

_____

_____

_____

Modern day totalitarianism has a softer approach than that of the Soviet Union. To what extent do you agree or disagree with this?

_____

_____

_____

_____

Have you ever been afraid or unable to express a different opinion from one held by the majority of people, and how were you able to deal with that situation?

_____

_____

_____

_____

_____

Can modern day Christians truly resist the effects of soft totalitarianism?

What does it mean for you to live in truth?

Have you ever had to accept a lie simply because it affords you convenience, and are you still living that lie or not?

_____

_____

_____

_____

Describe a situation where you have chosen pleasure over suffering for the faith.

_____

_____

_____

_____

_____

_____

_____

_____

_____

_____

_____

Personal Reflections

How This Chapter Made Me Feel

LESSONS LEARNED FROM THIS CHAPTER

_____
_____
_____
_____
_____
_____

HOW I INTEND TO APPLY LESSONS TO MY LIFE

_____
_____
_____
_____
_____

CHAPTER 2
OUR PRE-TOTALITARIAN CULTURE

IMPORTANT POINTS TO NOTE

➢ Faith, both in the Church and in the government, has been on a decline for several years, and its effects have begun to affect the way human beings observe and navigate the world.

➢ The Marxist theory appealed to the desires of people of Russia, leading them right into the arms of communism.

➢ Present day America and the prerevolutionary Russia have, in common, their inability to foresee the graveness of their acceptance of totalitarianism and communism.

➢ The interests and values of a nation's intellectuals and cultural Ellis are fundamental to the forward growth and direction of the said nation.

➢ Social justice warriors believe in taking power away from the oppressors and giving it to the oppressed.

➢ More American youths are abandoning their faith in the church and society, and this has created a divide amongst the people in the country.

QUESTIONS

Why is totalitarianism the right or wrong way to go for America as a nation?

_____
_____
_____
_____
_____
_____
_____
_____
_____

Social justice warriors do more harm than good to a nation. To what extents do you agree or disagree?

_____
_____
_____
_____
_____
_____
_____
_____

Why is it right or wrong to take away power from the oppressors and give it the oppressed?

_____
_____
_____
_____
_____
_____

Have you ever been attacked by social justice warriors, and how were you able to deal with that?

_____
_____
_____
_____

As a Christian, how has your faith been tested in the face of totalitarianism?

_____
_____
_____
_____
_____

Personal Reflections

How This Chapter Made Me Feel

LESSONS LEARNED FROM THIS CHAPTER

_____
_____
_____
_____
_____
_____
_____

HOW I INTEND TO APPLY LESSONS TO MY LIFE

_____
_____
_____
_____
_____

CHAPTER THREE
PROGRESSIVISM AS RELIGION

IMPORTANT POINTS TO NOTE
- Progress does not necessarily mean better.
- The Grand March is a march by the Leftists towards a belief of inevitable progress irrespective of obstacles trying to halt their stride.
- The approach towards progress is what separates the progressive directions of the Lefts from the Rights.
- Progress according to the Lefts requires a firm hold like the government charging them on and pushing them forward.
- While progress for the Rights is less dependent on the influence of the government.
- Progress without God isn't progress at all.
- Christians must affirm themselves with the truth in all they do.

QUESTIONS

What do you understand by the Myth of Progress?

_____
_____
_____
_____

Why is it important to follow the progressive directions of the Rights and not the Lefts?

_____

_____

_____

_____

_____

_____

_____

What are your individual goals towards progress both in the church and society?

_____

_____

_____

_____

_____

_____

_____

_____

_____

_____

_____

In finding God, what parts of yourself did you have to give up to truly seek Him out?

_____

_____

_____

_____

_____

_____

_____

_____

_____

Have you ever felt like your happiness and freedom are being obstructed, how did that make you feel?

_____

_____

_____

_____

_____

_____

_____

_____

Personal Reflections

How This Chapter Made Me Feel

LESSONS LEARNED FROM THIS CHAPTER

_____
_____
_____
_____
_____
_____

HOW I INTEND TO APPLY LESSONS TO MY LIFE

_____
_____
_____
_____
_____

CHAPTER FOUR
CAPITALISM, WOKE AND WATCHFUL

IMPORTANT POINTS TO NOTE

- Information, they say, is power, so we must be conscious of how much of our information we allow others access to.
- Surveillance is one of the strongest armors we constantly give the government and big companies access to through technological appliances such as smartphones, computers, and the internet at large.
- Technological advancement has helped boost the economy of our nation, and its achievements have been so grand, but we also cannot disregard the effects it has on the people.
- China has become one of the most advanced countries in the world in terms of technological advancements, yet with each advancement, its citizens lose just a little more freedom.
- China is proof that totalitarianism can still exist now.
- Government bodies such as the CIA can access information about anyone of interest to them very easily because of all the information they continually gather from us.

QUESTIONS

Have you ever considered how much information and data our phones collect from us on a daily basis?

_____
_____
_____

Are you on social media, Facebook, Instagram, etc, and how much information about you have you shared on each of them?

_____
_____
_____
_____
_____
_____

Do you normally live your life as though you are being watched by some Big Brother, and how does it make you feel?

_____
_____

Is it beneficial to you as a Christian and citizen of a nation to advance technologically at the expense of your privacy?

Do you believe America is gradually headed towards a similar fate as the Chinese, and why?

Personal Reflections

How This Chapter Made Me Feel

LESSONS LEARNED FROM THIS CHAPTER

_____
_____
_____
_____
_____
_____
_____

HOW I INTEND TO APPLY LESSONS TO MY LIFE

_____
_____
_____
_____
_____

PART TWO

How to Live in Truth

CHAPTER FIVE
VALUE NOTHING MORE THAN TRUTH

IMPORTANT POINTS TO NOTE

- Speaking up about the truth can turn you into a piranha.
- For most people, lies are more convenient. They tell themselves these lies because it is beneficial to them.
- The decision to stand by the truth is a decision one must choose to take, irrespective of whoever and whatever attempts to stand in the way.
- Truth is fundamental, and any country that doesn't make an effort to promote the truth is definitely pushing a lie to its citizens.
- Silence can be a very effective kind of resistance.
- A society's values are carried in the stories it chooses to tell about its people.

QUESTIONS

Are you willing to be cut off from everything and everyone you are familiar with for the sake of the truth?

_____
_____
_____

In what ways have you sacrificed your comfort by speaking the truth in gatherings that expect you to conform to their lies?

_____
_____
_____
_____
_____
_____

How do you, as a person who stands by the truth, live under totalitarianism?

_____
_____
_____
_____
_____
_____
_____
_____
_____

How do you choose when to speak up about a lie or when to simply stay mute?

_____
_____
_____
_____
_____
_____
_____
_____
_____

What have you risked standing by the truth?

_____
_____
_____
_____
_____
_____
_____
_____

Personal Reflections

How This Chapter Made Me Feel

LESSONS LEARNED FROM THIS CHAPTER

_____
_____
_____
_____
_____
_____
_____

HOW I INTEND TO APPLY LESSONS TO MY LIFE

_____
_____
_____
_____
_____

CHAPTER SIX
CULTIVATE CULTURAL MEMORY

KEY TAKEAWAYS & IMPORTANT POINTS TO NOTE

- One of the most effective ways of resisting totalitarianism is by keeping our histories alive.
- The present generation has lost touch with history so much that the disconnect has affected their judgement so immensely.
- Teaching the younger ones history preserves the memory and gives them a better understanding of how to resist the pressures of totalitarianism.
- Christians must ensure that in passing down history, they also pass down the faith, as this helps the younger ones become more grounded towards resisting totalitarianism.
- History and Christianity can be structured to seem more entertaining to the younger ones through literature, movies, plays etc.

QUESTIONS

How much do you know about your history?

_____
_____
_____
_____

Do you often feel disconnected from your history, and how has that affected your view of things on a vast level?

How often do you teach your younger ones or children your history and faith?

_____

_____

_____

_____

_____

How rich was the history you were taught in school, and how much did it help or not?

_____

_____

_____

_____

_____

_____

_____

_____

_____

_____

_____

_____

Personal Reflections

_____
_____
_____
_____
_____
_____
_____

How This Chapter Made Me Feel

_____
_____
_____
_____
_____

LESSONS LEARNED FROM THIS CHAPTER

_____
_____
_____
_____
_____
_____
_____

HOW I INTEND TO APPLY LESSONS TO MY LIFE

_____
_____
_____
_____
_____

CHAPTER SEVEN
FAMILIES ARE RESISTANCE CELLS

IMPORTANT POINTS TO NOTE

- Our first contact with the world is through our family. They are the bedrock upon which our knowledge of the world grows.
- Family bond was one of the strongest bonds for resisting totalitarianism.
- The Benda family bond was one of the strongest resistance bonds during the communist days of the Soviet Union.
- Christian families were mostly the bedrock upon which faithful resistance to communism was formed.
- The modern-day man has lost the conviction to fight to sustain their marriages.
- The rate of divorce in the world has spiked in the present day, and most people are not willing to make the effort to get through suffering, even in its most minimal state.

QUESTIONS

What does family mean to you?

_____

_____

_____

_____

_____

_____

How has your family strengthened your faith both in society and the church?

_____

_____

_____

_____

The Benda family and all the other brave families withstood the pressures of communism, to what extent can you and your family withstand the coming pressures of totalitarianism?

_____

_____

_____

_____

_____

_____

_____

What's your take on divorce and why?

_____
_____
_____
_____
_____
_____
_____
_____
_____
_____

What moral values have you learned from your family, in and how has it shaped who you are today?

_____
_____
_____
_____
_____
_____

Personal Reflections

How This Chapter Made Me Feel

LESSONS LEARNED FROM THIS CHAPTER

_____
_____
_____
_____
_____
_____

HOW I INTEND TO APPLY LESSONS TO MY LIFE

_____
_____
_____
_____
_____

CHAPTER EIGHT

RELIGION, THE BEDROCK OF RESISTANCE

IMPORTANT POINTS TO NOTE

- Religion is the rock upon which Christians must stand and resist.
- Religion offers an alternative worldview that can give hope to the hopeless and strength to the weak.
- Living in truth is the single most important aspect of true Christianity.
- We must embrace suffering and hardship as normal parts of choosing to resist the coming order.
- Our source of strength and truth must be the Bible. In it we must find true Truth.
- Our faith will still be critically tested, and only the strong Christians will persist to the end.
- Jesus suffered for a better world, and as Christians, if is our lot to embrace necessary suffering for a better world.

QUESTIONS

How has religion helped you get through a difficult time?

_____

_____

_____

_____

_____
_____
_____
_____
_____
_____
_____

Describe a situation where your faith helped you restore your hope and strength.

_____
_____
_____
_____
_____
_____
_____
_____

Have you lost a friend or job because you stood by a different opinion from theirs?

_____
_____

In what ways has your faith been tested, and how did you get through it?

_____
_____
_____
_____
_____
_____
_____
_____

Narrate a miracle that has happened to you or anyone close to you.

_____
_____
_____
_____
_____
_____
_____
_____
_____
_____

Personal Reflections

How This Chapter Made Me Feel

LESSONS LEARNED FROM THIS CHAPTER

_____
_____
_____
_____
_____
_____
_____

HOW I INTEND TO APPLY LESSONS TO MY LIFE

_____
_____
_____
_____
_____
_____

CHAPTER NINE
STANDING IN SOLIDARITY

IMPORTANT POINTS TO NOTE

- ➤ Small communities are groups created by believers to promote solidarity amongst Christians.
- ➤ Small communities are useful to create connections and generate a sense of resistance.
- ➤ They are safe spaces where people go to seek God.
- ➤ Solidarity must not only be exclusive to Christians. Seek out non-believers and create useful bonds with them.
- ➤ Liberal artists and writers help Christians understand the world beyond the church.
- ➤ No revolution can be made by one person.
- ➤ In solidarity, we find the strength and the spiritual and communal power to resist.

QUESTIONS

How acquainted are you with the small communities where you reside?

_____
_____
_____
_____
_____

_____

_____

_____

_____

What values do these small groups have for you?

_____

_____

_____

_____

_____

_____

_____

_____

_____

_____

What is your relationship like with non-Christians, and what lesson of solidarity have you learned from them?

_____

_____

_____

Have you ever converted a non-believer into the ways of the Lord, and how?

Personal Reflections

How This Chapter Made Me Feel

LESSONS LEARNED FROM THIS CHAPTER

_____
_____
_____
_____
_____
_____
_____

HOW I INTEND TO APPLY LESSONS TO MY LIFE

_____
_____
_____
_____
_____
_____

CHAPTER 10
THE GIFT OF SUFFERING

IMPORTANT POINTS TO NOTE

- Suffering, in all its trials, can be a learning process for us.
- Suffering teaches us a lesson, and we must allow ourselves to embrace suffering so that we can truly learn what it teaches us.
- To withstand the pressures of suffering, we must be followers of the Lord, and not admirers.
- As Christians, we must judge our suffering based on purpose.
- The value of suffering can only be recognized in its sanctification.
- The gospel today has been soiled by prosperity, with pastors preaching about worldly riches and success as opposed to the true values of suffering.
- Communal suffering can lead to spiritual strength and deep forgiveness.

QUESTIONS

How do you handle situations in which you suffer?

_____

_____

_____

_____
_____
_____
_____
_____
_____
_____
_____

How often do you choose pleasure over a time of necessary suffering?

_____
_____
_____
_____
_____
_____
_____

Are you an admirer or a follower of Christ?

_____
_____

What lessons have you learned from suffering for a purpose?

_____
_____
_____
_____
_____
_____
_____
_____

Have you ever suffered along with someone else, and how did the shared experience make you feel?

_____
_____
_____
_____
_____
_____

Personal Reflections

_____
_____
_____
_____
_____
_____
_____
_____

How This Chapter Made Me Feel

_____
_____
_____
_____
_____

LESSONS LEARNED FROM THIS CHAPTER

_____
_____
_____
_____
_____
_____
_____

HOW I INTEND TO APPLY LESSONS TO MY LIFE

_____
_____
_____
_____
_____
_____

Made in the USA
Monee, IL
26 March 2021